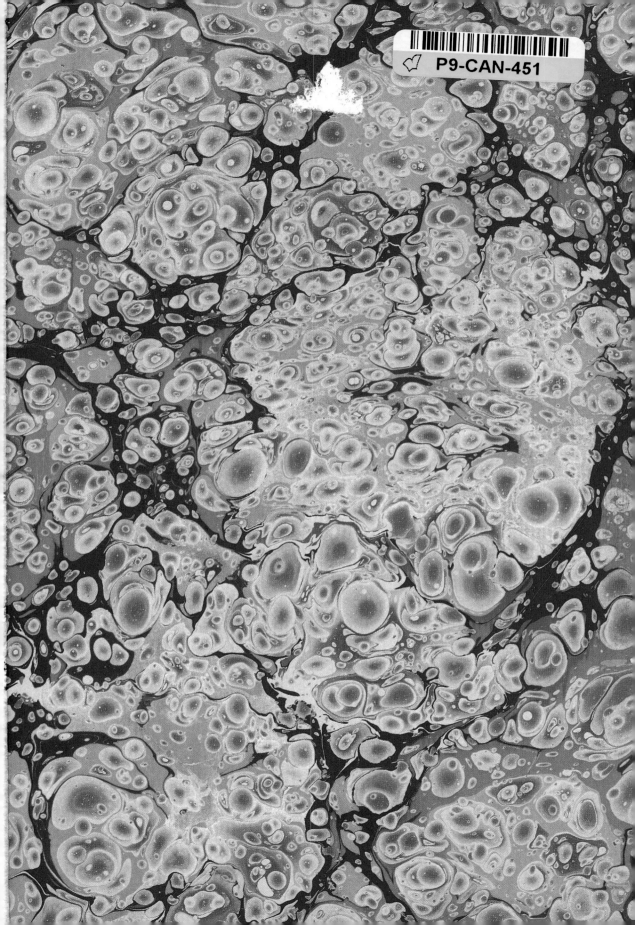

Days of Glory

A Gentleman's Chronicle

Chronicled by:

Original drawings of characters and events
of the American Civil War
by

Marshall Ausburn

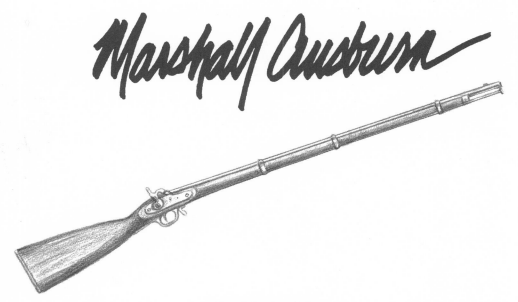

Published by
The Paint Box Studio Press • Marietta, Georgia 30064

ISBN: 0-9613287-4-6

Published and printed in the United States by

The Paint Box Studio Press
81 Whitlock Avenue
Marietta, GA 30064

(404)499-7299

10   9   8   7   6   5   4   3   2   1

About the Artist...

Georgia native, Marshall Ausburn became
fascinated with sketching Confederate
and Union soldiers after attending
weekend Civil War reenactments
at the Kennesaw Mountain Battle-
field near Atlanta. Camera in hand,
he was impressed by the devotion to
authenticity by these men and women

Marshall Ausburn, Artist

actors. They became compelling subjects for his talented pencil. He
further studied this time period through extensive reading. Among his
favorites were accounts by Union historian, Bruce Catton. The
drawings included in **Days of Glory, a Gentleman's Cronicle** are of
real people. Perhaps they will recognize themselves.

An artist since his high school years, Mr. Ausburn served four years in
the United States Navy as a torpedo technician until 1972. He then
attended Georgia State University on the GI Bill graduating with a
degree in American History.

Currently a full-time professional artist, Mr.Ausburn lives
in Marietta, Georgia with his wife and two teenage
daughters. He has exhibited and sold his works in galleries
and shows throughout the Southeast. Talented in a variety
of mediums and subjects, his works range from acrylics and
watercolors to cartooning and architectural renderings.

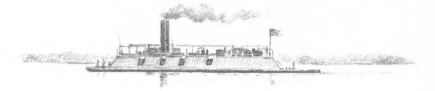

An interesting sidelight...the Ausburns discovered that their
great, great grandfather, James D. Ausburn served in the
War Between the States (as it is called in the South), with
the Georgia Volunteer Infantry. He Became a Private on
March 4, 1862, was captured during the defeat of
Vicksburg (Mississippi) July 4, 1863 and paroled three
days later. The last roll call he answered, according to
records, was February 29, 1864. It is rumored in the
Ausburn family that he might have taken his chances and
slipped off the Texas to seek fame, fortune, and to escape a
horrible war.

ivate James D. Ausburn

Tips and Uses for This Book

Webster's defines a chronicle as an "historical record of events in the order in which they happened." Now you can chronicle your life, your business calendar, your school assignments, your games and competitions, your appointments, your social life, even a brief journal. Whatever you wish.

This book is not dated so you can begin using it anytime. There are, however, a few things you'll need to do to get the book organized for your use. First, the title page has space for your name, the chronicler. Put down your beginning date, too. The book contains enough pages for a full year of your activities.

Each section begins with a month-at-a-glance, refer to the calendars at the back of the book and fill-in the upcoming month. Next, write-in the month and the name of the day on the seven-days-at-a-glance pages. Now, you are ready to make history!

"Life must be lived forward; but it can only be understood backwards." Kierkegaard

The Publisher hopes you enjoy these fine pencil drawings by artist and Civil War buff, Marshall Ausburn. If they spur further interest for you in the American Civil War, we hope you'll have an opportunity to not only visit your local library, but also explore other great resources for this tragic period in our United States history. There are solemn battlefields, museums filled with historic objects, colorful exhibits, towns and homes preserved for touring, movies, videos, and thousands of books---all waiting for you!

Orginally composed of all Scotch immigrants, The New York "Highlanders" fashioned themselves after the Cameron Highlanders of the British Army. Their full dress uniform of kilts lasted only as long as a great deal of derisive laughter and an influx of non-scotch recruits would allow.   After the first battle of Bull Run, the Highlanders were not pleased with the direction the war had taken and decided mutiny was the best course to follow.   General McClellan, who did not approve of mutiny, brought up a number of Army regulars and once these men loaded and aimed their rifles, the reluctant Scots were convinced life under Yankee command wasn't so bad after all.

Sunday	Monday	Tuesday	Wednesday	Thursday	Friday	Saturday

Notes

1

2

3

4

5

6

7

8

9

10

11

12

13

14

M*rs. Rose Greenhow, a Washington, D.C. socialite, whose suitors included senators, cabinet members, and an ex-president, was bold enough or foolish enough to run a rather obvious spy ring from her home on 16th street. Eventually, the Secret Service was forced to act and after months of "house arrest," she was sent to the Old Capitol Prison. Because of her very nervous, high placed friends, she was never hanged, but exiled to the South, leaving soon after for Europe as a diplomatic courier for Jefferson Davis. Returning home on a blockade runner with "important information" for Mr. Davis, her ship was intercepted by a Union gunboat and in an attempted escape, she drowned, weighted down by gold in her money belt.*

15

16

17

18

19

20

21

22

23

24

25

26

27

28

29

30

31

Notes

*O*ne of the first black regiments formed in the Civil War, the 54th Landed on Morris Island, South Carolina feeling they had a great deal to prove. This spit of sand outside of Charleston Harbor was the home of Battery Wagner, a fortress of palmetto logs and sand bags that would resist 8 weeks of assault and Naval bombardment, only falling into Union hands when it's defenders felt there was no longer any reason to stay. The 54th had their turn on July 18, 1863, as one of the leading regiments in a head on assault. What they wound up proving was they could stand up and be slaughtered as well as any white soldier. More than 40% of the regiment was shot to pieces and buried in shallow graves along with their white commander, Colonel Robert Gould Shaw.

SUNDAY	MONDAY	TUESDAY	WEDNESDAY	THURSDAY	FRIDAY	SATURDAY

Notes

_____
_____
_____
_____
_____
_____
_____
_____
_____
_____
_____
_____
_____
_____
_____

1

2

3

4

5

6

7

8

9

10

11

12

13

14

*B*lack regiments almost always served with distinction throughout the Civil War, earning 23 Congressional Medals of Honor, but they faced immense handicaps. It took the United States Congress two years after authorizing their formation to allow them equal pay with their white counterparts. When they were captured by Confederates in battle, they were generally shot or sold into slavery. Perhaps the rarest of all Civil War reunions was that of a few black survivors of Andersonville prison.

15

16

17

18

19

20

21

22

23

24

25

26

27

28

29

30

31

Notes

For the first three years of the war, the Shenandoah Valley of Virginia was the Confederate Bread Basket and all Union attempts at disrupting this were soundly defeated. In 1864, however, things changed. J.E.B. Stuart was dead and the North finally found a cavalry commander worth his salt in Phil Sheridan. Sheridan was a hard man. He found infamy in the Indian Wars of the 1870's with his quote, "The only good Indian is a dead Indian." General Grant ordered Sheridan to turn the valley into "a barren waste...so that crows flying over it for the balance of the season will have to carry their provender with them." This he did to the satisfaction (or dissatisfaction) of all concerned.

SUNDAY	MONDAY	TUESDAY	WEDNESDAY	THURSDAY	FRIDAY	SATURDAY

Notes

1

2

3

4

5

6

7

8

9

10

11

12

13

14

The American Civil War did more than temporarily split a nation, it also divided many families. It was very often, literally brother against brother, not to mention, son-in-law versus father-in-law and father against son. Frederick Hubbard of the New Orleans Artillery and his brother Henry of the 1st Minnesota Infantry had not seen each other in six years until their reunion laying side-by-side in hospital beds after the first Battle of Manassas.

15

16

17

18

19

20

21

22

23

24

25

26

27

28

29

30

31

Notes

*J*ohnny Clem of Ohio ran away to war at age nine. After many refusals, the 22nd Michigan accepted him as a mascot and drummer, even giving him a musket whittled down to his size. Clem participated in most of the major engagements of the war with the 22nd and earned fame as the "drummer boy of Chicamauga" after he reportedly shot and killed a rebel demanding his surrender. After the war he was refused admission into West Point, but was eventually commissioned a 2nd Lieutenant, retiring in 1916 as a Major General.

SUNDAY	MONDAY	TUESDAY	WEDNESDAY	THURSDAY	FRIDAY	SATURDAY

Notes

1

2

3

4

5

6

7

8

9

10

11

12

13

14

*O*n July 4, 1863, the Confederate commander of Vicksburg, Pennsylvanian, John C. Pemberton, surrendered his command to General Grant, ending a seige of 47 days. The civilians and soldiers of Vicksburg had been living in dugouts and caves because of the almost constant bombardment by Union artillery and ironclads in the Mississippi River. Since the only commodity the Rebels had plenty of was hunger, mule meat, rats, and house pets became standard fare. Even though the Yankees were gracious in victory, actually cheering the Rebel defenders, it was a long time before the 4th of July was celebrated as a holiday in Vicksburg, Mississippi.

15

16

17

18

19

20

21

22

23

24

25

26

27

28

29

30

31

Notes

*O*ne of the problems with the Southern Confederacy was that Southern loyalty, very often, rested not with the Confederacy or even to individual states, but with families and communities. One such instance was in Jones County, Mississippi, where the Confederate conscription, confiscation, and taxation laws proved to be entirely too much for shoemaker, Newton Knight. He formed the "Republic of Jones" and with eighty or so recruits, began a bloody Robin Hood style operation against the Confederate government. There was a lot of popular support for Knight, but not within the Confederate army, which spent a great deal of effort and bloodshed trying to suppress him. They were never completely successful and in the end Knight survived, neither tried nor punished.

SUNDAY	MONDAY	TUESDAY	WEDNESDAY	THURSDAY	FRIDAY	SATURDAY

Notes

1

2

3

4

5

6

7

8

9

10

11

12

13

14

*T*he scarcity of food was a constant Southern problem for civilians as well as soldiers. There were many instances of hoarding and women rioting against high prices. The soldiers generally ate what they could find, frequently hard corn intended for their horses. In a letter to his sister, Texan G. L. Robertson tells of eating roasted armadillo, which he found "to be very fine...Far superior to any possum meat I ever eat."

15

16

17

18

19

20

21

22

23

24

25

26

27

28

29

30

31

Notes

Like most wars, the American Civil War was a great proving- ground for new ways of killing more people. Machine guns, ironclads, and submarines were introduced during this period. A somewhat more dubious achievement was the Union Parrott fifle, known as the "Swamp Angel" Fired at night from the swamps of southwest Charleston, South Carolina, the cannon hurled 200 pound incendiary shells into the city with the intention of setting Charlestown afire. The Confederate commmander, General P.G.T. Beauregard protested this firing into a city "filled with sleeping women and children." The General was ignored, but Charleston was not set on fire and the Swamp Angel exploded after only 36 shots fired.

SUNDAY	MONDAY	TUESDAY	WEDNESDAY	THURSDAY	FRIDAY	SATURDAY

Notes

_____
_____
_____
_____
_____
_____
_____
_____
_____
_____
_____
_____
_____

1

2

3

4

5

6

7

8

9

10

11

12

13

14

On the day after the people of Virginia voted for secession, Union troops moved to take over the city of Alexandria. As the soldiers entered the city, their 24 year old commander, Colonel Elmer Ellsworth, a former member of Abe Lincoln's law firm, spotted a rebel flag flying over the Marshall House Inn. Ellsworth quickly got to the roof and removed the flag, but as he was coming back downstairs, the innkeeper, James W. Jackson killed Ellsworth with a shotgun blast to the chest. An aide killed Jackson and suddenly the country had two martyrs.

15

16

17

18

19

20

21

22

23

24

25

26

27

28

29

30

31

Notes

*T*he minie ball, the bullet of choice in the Civil War, was the invention of Captain C. E. Minié of France. Its' distinguishing feature was a hollow base which caused the bullet to expand when fired, increasing force and accuracy of the spinning hot lead. This in turn was a boon to the makers of surgical knives and saws, because when a soldier was hit by a minie ball and it struck a bone, it did not just break the bone, it shattered and destroyed it.

SUNDAY	MONDAY	TUESDAY	WEDNESDAY	THURSDAY	FRIDAY	SATURDAY

Notes

1

2

3

4

5

6

7

8

9

10

11

12

13

14

All American wars have stories of elderly men attempting and failing to enlist in the Army. In the Civil War, elderly men attempted and were enlisted in the armies of both sides. The 37th Iowa Infantry, "The Gray Beards," had 145 soldiers 60 years old or older. The oldest, Private Curtis King enlisted at 80, but served only six months.

15

16

17

18

19

20

21

22

23

24

25

26

27

28

29

30

31

Notes

A brigade of 1500 men, left as a rear guard during Sherman's March to the Sea, were dug in at a fine defensive position facing the town of Griswoldville, Georgia. They were soon suprised to see a contingent of Georgia Militia march through town and assemble for attack. The militia came forward in traditonal close order formation and were easily repulsed. They did this twice more and were twice more beaten back before limping off toward Macon. In the field after the fight, the cheering Yankees discovered to their horror, the 600 dead and wounded soldiers laying about them were composed entirely of old men and young boys. From a diary of a member of the 103rd Illinois Volunteer Infantry *"I was never so affected at the sight of dead and wounded before. I hope I will never have to shoot at such men again."*

SUNDAY	MONDAY	TUESDAY	WEDNESDAY	THURSDAY	FRIDAY	SATURDAY

Notes

1

2

3

4

5

6

7

8

9

10

11

12

13

14

In a letter to his wife, Georgian T. W. Montfort does not mince words in describing his feeling for the Northern invaders. "Teach my children to hate them with that bitter hatred that will never permit them to meet under any circumstances without seeking to destroy each other. I know the breach is now wide and deep between us and the Yankees let it widen and deepen until all Yankees or no Yankees are to live in the South."

15

16

17

18

19

20

21

22

23

24

25

26

27

28

29

30

31

Notes

*F*raternization and trading with the enemy was a constant irritant to officers of both sides. Trading was usually Rebel tobacco for Yankee coffee, but anything and everything, especially newspapers were swapped. Exchanges often took place by rivers dividing the two armies and the articles were sent across on small handmade sailboats. During periods of lull between battles, the rivers often took on the appearance of miniature regattas.

SUNDAY	MONDAY	TUESDAY	WEDNESDAY	THURSDAY	FRIDAY	SATURDAY

Notes

1

2

3

4

5

6

7

8

9

10

11

12

13

14

The Virginia wilderness was an appropriately named spot. The foilage was so thick, sunshine was a rare commodity. When men fought, they seldom saw who they were fighting and when they fell, as they did in prodigious numbers, they were often consumed in the fires racing through the dry leaves and underbrush. Beginning with this battle between The Army of the Potomac and The Army of Northern Virginia on May 5, 1864, until the surrender at Appomatox on April 9, 1865, men of these armies were killed every day. Some days were wholesale slaughter, somedays, death was a more random chance, but everyday soldiers died and families wept.

15

16

17

18

19

20

21

22

23

24

25

26

27

28

29

30

31

Notes

*W*hen *Sherman took Atlanta, he told the residents they had ten days to evacuate, because he planned to set fire to their city. Mayor James M. Calhoun protested against this, particularly the hardship of moving the aged and infirm. Sherman agreed this was indeed hard, but "You cannot qualify war in harsher terms than I will. War is cruelty and you cannot refine it...You might as well appeal against the thunderstorm as against these terrible hardships of war."*

SUNDAY	MONDAY	TUESDAY	WEDNESDAY	THURSDAY	FRIDAY	SATURDAY

Notes

1

2

3

4

5

6

7

8

9

10

11

12

13

14

Sherman said his march to the sea was made in order to "make Georgia howl." This he accomplished and his men seemed to have a fine time doing it. A "bummer" with the 143rd New York Volunteers wrote home-"we had a gay old campaign, destroyed all we could not eat, stole their niggers, burned and twisted their roads, and raised hell generally."

15

16

17

18

19

20

21

22

23

24

25

26

27

28

29

30

31

Notes

To both new, citizen armies, as with all armies before and after, drill was the prescription for turning individuals into soldiers. However, in the Civil War there was a distinct shortage of trained drill instructors. Teenage military cadets and foreign soldiers were often used, but sometimes they just had to "wing it". Passing in review in front of a general, the 8th Wisconsin Infantry was due to make a right turn, but their commander could not remember the command for column right. At the last moment, the exasperated officer came out with, "GEE! God damn it, GEE!" and the column of former farmers turned sharply right.

SUNDAY	MONDAY	TUESDAY	WEDNESDAY	THURSDAY	FRIDAY	SATURDAY

Notes

1

2

3

4

5

6

7

8

9

10

11

12

13

14

(Note: misspellings and capital letters appear in original)

*B*oth Northerners and Southerners felt God was on their side, perhaps none so virulently as the writer in **Louisiana's Magnolia Plantation Record Book** *"This day is set a part by President Jefferson Davis for fasting & praying...My Prayer sincerely to God is that Every Black Republican in the Hole combined whorl Either man woman o chile that is opposed to negro slavery...shal be trubled with pestilents & calamitys of all Kinds & Dragout the Balance of there existence in misray & Degradation with scarsely food & rayment enought to keep sole & Body together...amen."*

15

16

17

18

19

20

21

22

23

24

25

26

27

28

29

30

31

Notes

On May 9, 1864 both armies were dug in around Spotsylvania, Virginia and to keep things from getting dull, sharpshooters were looking for anything that moved. General John Sedgwick noticed his men ducking and flinching at the periodic sound of gunfire coming from 800 yards away. He chided them saying, "They couldn't hit an elephant at this distance." Those were his last words. The next shot caught him below his left eye.

SUNDAY	MONDAY	TUESDAY	WEDNESDAY	THURSDAY	FRIDAY	SATURDAY

Notes

1

2

3

4

5

6

7

8

9

10

11

12

13

14

The 1864 Confederate victory at New Market, Virginia is remembered in the South primarily for the participation of 247 teenage, Virginia Military Institute cadets. Before the battle, the cadets, in their snappy parade uniforms, had been greeted by the Confederate veterans with laughter and a band playing "Rockabye Baby." After a complete rout of the Union forces, in which the cadets lost nearly a quarter of their ranks, the veterans changed their tune. The teenagers had not won the battle all by themselves, as some accounts of the day would claim, but they had served gallantly.

15

16

17

18

19

20

21

22

23

24

25

26

27

28

29

30

31

Notes

Notes

Notes

1992

JANUARY
MAY
SEPTEMBER
FEBRUARY
JUNE
OCTOBER
MARCH
JULY
NOVEMBER
APRIL
AUGUST
DECEMBER

1993

JANUARY
MAY
SEPTEMBER
FEBRUARY
JUNE
OCTOBER
MARCH
JULY
NOVEMBER
APRIL
AUGUST
DECEMBER

1994

JANUARY
MAY
SEPTEMBER
FEBRUARY
JUNE
OCTOBER
MARCH
JULY
NOVEMBER
APRIL
AUGUST
DECEMBER

1995

JANUARY
MAY
SEPTEMBER
FEBRUARY
JUNE
OCTOBER
MARCH
JULY
NOVEMBER
APRIL
AUGUST
DECEMBER

1996

JANUARY
MAY
SEPTEMBER
FEBRUARY
JUNE
OCTOBER
MARCH
JULY
NOVEMBER
APRIL
AUGUST
DECEMBER

1997

JANUARY
MAY
SEPTEMBER
FEBRUARY
JUNE
OCTOBER
MARCH
JULY
NOVEMBER
APRIL
AUGUST
DECEMBER

1998

JANUARY
MAY
SEPTEMBER
FEBRUARY
JUNE
OCTOBER
MARCH
JULY
NOVEMBER
APRIL
AUGUST
DECEMBER

1999

JANUARY
MAY
SEPTEMBER
FEBRUARY
JUNE
OCTOBER
MARCH
JULY
NOVEMBER
APRIL
AUGUST
DECEMBER

2000

JANUARY
MAY
SEPTEMBER
FEBRUARY
JUNE
OCTOBER
MARCH
JULY
NOVEMBER
APRIL
AUGUST
DECEMBER

2001

JANUARY	MAY	SEPTEMBER
FEBRUARY	JUNE	OCTOBER
MARCH	JULY	NOVEMBER
APRIL	AUGUST	DECEMBER

2002

JANUARY	MAY	SEPTEMBER
FEBRUARY	JUNE	OCTOBER
MARCH	JULY	NOVEMBER
APRIL	AUGUST	DECEMBER

2003

JANUARY	MAY	SEPTEMBER
FEBRUARY	JUNE	OCTOBER
MARCH	JULY	NOVEMBER
APRIL	AUGUST	DECEMBER

2004

JANUARY	MAY	SEPTEMBER
FEBRUARY	JUNE	OCTOBER
MARCH	JULY	NOVEMBER
APRIL	AUGUST	DECEMBER

2005

JANUARY	MAY	SEPTEMBER
FEBRUARY	JUNE	OCTOBER
MARCH	JULY	NOVEMBER
APRIL	AUGUST	DECEMBER

2006

JANUARY	MAY	SEPTEMBER
FEBRUARY	JUNE	OCTOBER
MARCH	JULY	NOVEMBER
APRIL	AUGUST	DECEMBER

2007

JANUARY	MAY	SEPTEMBER
FEBRUARY	JUNE	OCTOBER
MARCH	JULY	NOVEMBER
APRIL	AUGUST	DECEMBER

2008

JANUARY	MAY	SEPTEMBER
FEBRUARY	JUNE	OCTOBER
MARCH	JULY	NOVEMBER
APRIL	AUGUST	DECEMBER

2009

JANUARY	MAY	SEPTEMBER
FEBRUARY	JUNE	OCTOBER
MARCH	JULY	NOVEMBER
APRIL	AUGUST	DECEMBER

Order Form for Paint Box Products

*To order books with a name beautifully hand-lettered by a professional calligrapher, send that name and payment (check, money order, VISA or Master Card) to **The Paint Box Studio Press** (Canadian orders-US Dollars only)*

Please allow 4 weeks for delivery.
Days of Glory, a Gentleman's Chronicle *(planner)* $14.95
Days of Glory, *14 notecards and envelopes* *6.00*
With Love From My Kitchen, *Country Edition (for recipes)* *18.95*
With Love From My Kitchen, *Victorian Edition (for recipes)*..................*18.95*
Roses in December *(write life story)* *14.95*
Welcome to My Kitchen, *(menu planner)* *11.95*
Recipe Cards *(20 assorted)* *3.00*

Please send me:

_____

_____

_____

Name for cover (books only)

_____

(please print)

Cost of personalizing..................................$ 3.00
Shipping, one book.................................... 2.00
Shipping, each additional book...................... .50
Shipping, each package notecards...................1.00
Shipping, each package recipe cards................ .30

(Georgia residents please add 5% sales tax)

Address for mailing label:

_____

_____

_____

Charge card #   MasterCard VISA   Exp. date

_____

Signature

_____

Phone # (in case we have questions
about your order, we need the number
of the person placing this order)

_____   **The Paint Box Studio Press**
81 Whitlock Avenue
Marietta, GA 30064
(404)499-7299 and FAX (404)427-5704

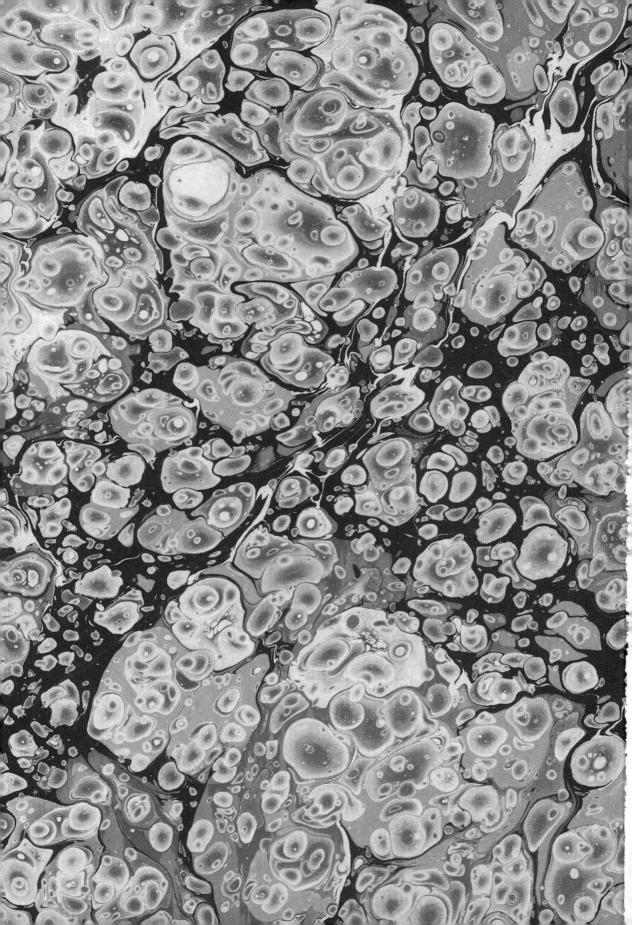